Busy Being Born

200 7-76

Copyright ©1974 by Todd Gitlin

All rights reserved including the right to reproduce any portion of this book in any form or by any means without prior written permission by the Publisher, excepting brief quotations used in connection with reviews or essays written specifically for inclusion in a magazine or newspaper.

The author gratefully acknowledges permission to reprint the following: "Wallace Shot," "Traffic Lights," and "Trembling," reprinted by permission of *The Nation,* copyright ©1972, 1973; "Homage to Paul Goodman," reprinted by permission of *The New York Review of Books,* copyright ©1972; "The Seventies," "After," "Nixon," "The McGovern Campaign," "The Defeated," and "Hiatus," reprinted by permission of *The Village Voice.* Copyright by The Village Voice, Inc., ©1972, 1973.

Library of Congress Catalog Card Number: 73-88273
ISBN: 0/87932/073/7

First Printing

Straight Arrow Books
625 Third Street
San Francisco, CA 94107

Distributed by Quick Fox Inc.
33 West 60th Street
New York, NY 10023

Order number: 102073

Production by Planned Production
Printed in the United States of America

Photographs by Justin Baird

For all of you who have been with me in the delivery room.

Words

My Friends
13 My Friends
13 After
14 Homage to Paul Goodman
15 To the Autobiographer
16 The Revisitor
17 The Final Solution
18 Friend
19 Man on a Mountain
20 Still Life: Fruit, Slippers, Fingers
21 Nietzsche in the Auschwitz Library
22 To My Enemy
23 Rejoining the Circle

See America First
25 Cloud on Twin Peaks
26 Over the Bay Bridge
27 The Sky Downtown
28 In Mendocino County
29 Morning in Santa Barbara
29 Through Wyoming
31 Big Thompson River
32 Trail Ridge Road, Rocky Mountain National Park
33 New York on a Mild Day
34 Through Nevada

Outside as Inside
35 What's the Matter America
38 The General's Nightmare
39 Oobie Doobie
40 "U.S. Attempted to Ignite Vietnam Forests in '66-67"
42 Wallace Shot
43 Nixon
44 The McGovern Campaign
45 The Defeated
46 Hiatus
47 The Seventies
48 The Chief Samurai
49 Two Aging Revolutionaries Meet in a Cafe: Fragment

Break-up
50 Loneliness
51 Abortions
52 Fault
52 Five Days Gone

53 I See Us at a Back Table
54 The Abandoned Ones Speak of Their Distant Lovers

"We May Not Have Much Time," Said He
56 "We May Not Have Much Time," Said He
57 July Night
58 The Texture of Kumquats
59 Afternoon
60 Ten Movements
62 Autumn
62 Diving
63 A Poem for You in Black and White
64 Shadows, Rivers

Prologue to Living in the Present
65 On the Edge
66 In the Desert, Almost Doomed
67 Poem Beginning with "But"
68 The Old Stadium
70 How Long
71 Praying in the Bathroom
72 Traffic Lights
72 Foundation
73 Functions of Imagination
74 After Newton: Ideological Fruit
75 Trembling
75 Now
76 The Cave
77 Water
78 Anatomy of Quiet
79 Lover

Caterpillar and Butterfly
80 Ambition
81 The Ambassador from Misery Shuffles His Feet under the Bargaining Table
82 The Animal Reunion
83 Sisyphus' Dream
85 The Hitchhiker Revolts
87 The Day the Clouds Fell
88 The Men
89 Seeking
89 The Return of the Repressed
90 Caterpillar and Butterfly
91 Turning Thirty

Words

When a pit opens and the great hands of the world push, and I can't stand, and I fall into myself, I stab the wall with words, and hope they harden into pitons.

Where are the words that rise and flutter lovely as a flag with one yellow star? Words that refuse to recant, that march to the wall singing "We Shall Overcome" as the sun pours into itself? Words as ivy on that wall? Words that flame like ever-replenishing fireworks, like flares not bombs? Words of fuel filling the empty engines? Words that the wino guzzles, content, and words that inflame the neatly partitioned hearts? Words of everyday dishrag hope, and the hope that ignites the stars? Words that inhabit the flimsy snowed-in cabin of lost experience, like a lantern? Words that open a trap door in the barbed roof, under a spray of stars?

When enough is never enough, when the missing pieces usurp the rest of the puzzle, when absences carve vast shapes and I live inside the shapes, the smooth walls, the passages swallowing passages, here are the words.

And here are curdled words snaking their way to the plane of the body. Hands along a spine and everything that happens between. The credible smoothness of skin. Incredible fusions of words like bodies, becoming themselves and other than themselves. Words that soar from the tangled sheets. Words that love their way into the unswept corners, the bloody barracks, the rusty syringes, the feverish eyes. Words that warm their way into the sealed lids. Words that crochet into a vest of music and become the colors. Words that gather in a soft circle singing remembered songs. Reminders to love life, reminders that become life. Incantations before the fire: when the door opens into another space, they break into laughter and welcome company. Despair is at home here, despair ensconces itself and is startled by joy flying up from the hinge of the split soul.

The wings of despair land on this same earth. The wings of despair are clumsy but also transportation. Delusions of madness rattle the grave apartments. Dark waves of anger break into churning light. Words that sound like the midnight undermoon shore. Words that mark boundaries and overlap them. Far out words, close in words.

Castles of ashes, and ashes becoming flesh. Words for rescinded dreams glinting in the dust. Words that ascend through smokestacks of worn passion, and burn into the sun. Words that glisten on an evening face in the heavy fog. Words that stun like polyhedral light behind glasses within the fog. Silences glowing within the fog, and words that stop the ornate clock.

If I am reborn as a word, may it be on the right lips, whatever the word.

Words for wounds, the only things unwounded. Words of reprieve to a man dying of cancer on Death Row. Words for the trees, the grass fragrant around Auschwitz, around My Lai.

Words that if not sung would lie fat and heavy around the heart. Words that poke like a white cane: where? At least across the street. Let's grind the bitter husk to grain, for someone's hunger.

And words steaming from the housewife's hot and bitter iron. Words that slice through jewelry-store windows. Words that explode in the soft suburbs. Words that embitter the daiquiri. Words that saw through the bars of the buffalo's cage.

Words in their own seasons, I speak. Friends, I am not responsible for a long winter. And yet I would speak Harpo's words, and none other.

May these words wind with grace around your waist, and walk, not stagger, to their page, their fate, behind your eyes, your ears.

My Friends

My Friends

Lights seeming to flicker on the hillside.

After

for Steve and Anne

After the movie the intermission.
After the battles the small New Hampshire town.
After the swollen hopes the small child.
After the red flag the town green,
    the sampler on the wall: "Don't tread on me."

Homage to Paul Goodman

Jewish Yankee,
citizen of a nation not yet born,

architect of unadorned castles,
assembling his ragtag crew without tools,

his rambling army without weapons, never for hire,
his university in the kitchen,

crocheting samplers of Reason to hang on the wall
instead of diplomas,

practicing simple delights of grey cloth
properly woven,

plucking an abacus
in the cluttered library.

Corrupter of youth, city's peripatetic,
grim lover

tilting at office buildings,
cranky uncle who never approved

and had to be consulted,
who helped me grow up

a little less absurd.
It will not be a matter of disciples,

more the original meaning of "gone to seed"
for the man who walked alone

dourly whistling a song I can't get out of my mind
even after he has vanished around the corner.

To the Autobiographer

for Ellie

You stand poised high over your life:
fetid green things of swamp,
the present as mirror of the past.

At the bottom of a distance you recognize yourself.
But is this the time to dive
headlong into the stench?—

Your legs are tired of running.
You have conspired to be here.
The distance ripples like some clearer moving water.

A deep breath beckons the moment,
the moment waits, will not renege.

Your heart moves into your legs
which push your head down,

                              down,
dragging distance with you through the air.
The past flies toward your face,
motion conquers the stench,
the mirror breaks into dark blossoms.

Underneath, released like minnows
among the tangled roots, your limbs
invent freedom between the lessons.
You swim in the clean water beneath,
before the past, until it is time—

now it is time to burst into the present light of sun.

The Revisitor

Long ago, when he was heavy with purpose,
the town was an ivy-bordered blank screen
on which he projected a tall hungry shadow
and animal heads from center stage. He walked
seeking a bloody altar under the bright lights.
Admirers paid the ultimate tribute: scorn.
Under the ancient clock he walked
importantly in straight lines, hands behind in a firm grip
balancing eyes ahead, aware—without needing to look—
of priests on the edge of their seats
who cheered and chanted:
                              "You! First born, first
                                  among equals,
First Amendment, first circle, first
principles, first in war, first
in peace, first, first. . . ."
                              He bowed.
They spoke: "Go out into the world.
Shake the world and preserve the faith.
Make the world yours and therefore ours. Make the world—"
and stabbed his chest with medals
and wiped his tears with parchment.

He sat in leather solace, sipped sherry,
recited the mantra, savored the sourball taste,
and buried it in a time capsule beneath his heart.

The surface wears away, he uncovers the capsule.
And when he returns to stalk the town
the ivy is thicker with shining barbs,
the screen is littered with cobblestone streets
and shops full of oddly colored,
intricately cut scrolls, and the priests
applaud new acts in the classical style.
He casts no shadow. The shadow is all the altar's.

The town thrives under the old clock, he is the ghost,
he haunts the town, lost in the wings in a revolving door
screaming about a wound that does not heal.

The Final Solution

In the dead heat of living with only direction
and no presence, or presence that nullifies direction
and answers questions with questions,
or directions that seem directionless,

in the crossroads confusion of back streets,
the cloverleaf malaise of twisted highway,
in the throb of blisters and the pinch of shoes,
the long afternoon between faces,

with crowds moaning past her bedroom window
and closed doors more common than faces;
with a keyring jangling around her neck—
in the long grey day of the soul

she wants to simplify her life:
contemplates a permanent, understands
it is only the wrong name for a hair-job;
contemplates a new pair of shoes (but there is already

a closetful), a new map (but the city
is the same), a new city (but the map
is the same): she wants to simplify
her life!—cuts off her feet.

Friend

for Barbara

Those fingers, those sweet claws
of need, caress of thin slivers,
you ask why I bleed, you're bleeding too,
who scratched first, it doesn't

matter, all that's real
is the blood, when we have what we want
it vanishes, the claws sprout, what do we want,
a certain sweetness, blood,

no, what else, a simple bead of joy
glistening on the long elastic
long bare string of this life, this life
is a therapy for this life,

no, it's not enough to fingerpaint
with the stuff of our own guts
or carve our portraits in the faces of friends,
why do we do this to each other,

at least we want to touch life to the cheek
since it can't be eaten, it can't be gotten inside,
here we are in the mud of I, hold me, I'll take you
down and you'll return the favor, no,

slow down, it won't be this way forever
though we are stones chipping the chisels
of advice and solace, enough right now to weep
and pool our tears in a small puddle of enoughness,

acid melting the claws

Man on a Mountain

Above timber, above the life
that manages and is managed down below,

above the likely limits of the flood
he scans the horizon for a revoked shore.

He sees abandoned shelves of books circling the peaks
and is breathed by air of expired incarnations.

The stench of tear gas floats in one nostril. . . .
The mountains will not descend into the life:

will not line the life with tiny flowers,
will not fill the hollow cabinet of the abandoned life.

He feels not quite faint and remembers broken bones
and the task—the task—what was the task?

The slowly grown lid of discipline
over the twisted oily rags of passion—

the skill: that's it, the skill,
his ticket in the Meaning lottery,

his skill: what was it again? Yes,
he will conduct group therapy on the ark

so that the couples may some day live in peace—
but he doesn't believe the couples should live in peace—

what was it he believed? In storming the mountain—
in storming the ark—in storming.

                                      He's sick of it:
he tries to lock the air inside his lungs:

he wants to make a statement with his life
but all the keys are punctuation marks.

Still Life: Fruit, Slippers, Fingers

Grandpa. Dead in the lungs.
Too many hours waiting
in your fruit and vegetable store.
Too many days, Grandpa, waiting
with yellow fingers.
                          When they came for you,
Sh'ma Israel, I didn't hear the siren,
didn't what-they-call understand
                                    and anyway
we never found the same words. Those Passover words
didn't work. I didn't hear.
You didn't ask. I never heard you ask
for anything but your slippers. Grandma
took good care.
                      Why ask?
Ask whom? Ask Herzl's portrait
in the foyer? Sons and daughters
on the way out through the hall? Ikons
of a dead Czar? Ask whom for what?
Ask in the *shul* around the corner. Ask again,
again, from the same books, the same questions,
the same answers.

The children should be happy, enough.
Enough, enough. *Dayenu.*

Too many Camels, Grandpa.

I remember stripping the pods
from the sweet peas. You shy at the scales.
"The nectarines are nice."
"Nice. Yes. I'll take a pound."
The tiny store. Closet of fresh things.
Wooden floor. Spaces between the slats.
Fruit. Sweeter peas. The best.
Your store. You don't know the next-door market
swallowed your store. Linoleum.
Selling gold fillings and fingernails
and Camel Filters.

They don't come for fruit any more.
Grandpa, they don't come. The supermarket fruit
tastes, these days, like shit.

Life. Enough. Still
life. Here, Grandpa. A nectarine. Delicious.

Nietzsche in the Auschwitz Library

The loveliest necklace of words
is a memo passed on by a man
who wants my neck.

Words of comfort
confirm my cancerous throat.

Words of command
incite my ridiculous rebel.

Lucidity is a bubble
indistinguishable within the froth.

Gentle words
inspire my grim reaper
of motives.

Words of wisdom
fester in my wound.

Words of knowledge
fatten me for the kill.

If words could heal
Webster would walk on water
and would be living here.

Language is not the body.
After the mind is force-fed
the body is barely the body.

A wad of words in my cheek.
I need a spittoon.

Dogs bark at passing cars.
Not knowing how to bark, I pass my days
watching for stars at high noon.

To My Enemy

My mind is scarred with thoughts
of you, and thoughts that might as well be of you.

You there with the whip,
you, turn around, you
with knives scabbarded in your ankles,
you with the barbed fingernails, you
with your arms dark-flaming.

Ah! Your face is a plain-framed mirror
throwing my teeth at me, my white troops
trapped between trenches of grimace and smile.

Dispassionately you observe
my kicking and screaming.
When I step out at you, you vanish,
leaving your Cheshire whip, flashing.

The calf, my leader, is gone, all that remains
is his stiffened, guaranteed Made-in-USA
hide, with teeth, on my milkfed mind.

My fault, then, for having solid skin.

This is the season for liquefaction,
flesh dissolving under the slicing edge
to reunite on the other side
in the vast waters beyond the hills

of threat, and if I succeed and my mind
becomes the ever-returning bottomless ocean,
lash, lash away, leave your stripes
on the waves if you can.

Rejoining the Circle

for Peggy Clark

We are sponges mopping the ever-replenishing
soot of the world, I thought, eying the dance
as I greeted old friends with news, gossip,
brave jokes—sponges who need parties,
dancing two by two, really one
by one by one . . . maybe a fleeting
tribe, squeezing ourselves out
into separate limbs and hips—

                            this I thought,
sitting it out—

                    and when
out of their singular graces
my friends formed the logic, the circle, and spun
around the implicit hub, I watched
from outside, restive detached point
from which the circle is seen
small and whole and continuous—

I thought of the ghost dance, the
desperate glad revival
of all we had meant to do,
had meant to be; I wondered
what is the hub, the premise,
where are the buffalo—

until, spinning past me, you reached
for my hand—
         my hand chose, the rest of me
followed—
         and opened a place for my feet,
which learned soon enough to kick
in time, as the circle contracted
like an anemone, in-folded and swelled,
never too big to burst the curve
of hands;
         smiles held, each of us pure water
reflected in pools of other
smiles—
         we danced to the beat, wouldn't you know,
of Tina Turner, "Working Together
We Can Make a Change,"
                      and I believed it.

See America First

Cloud on Twin Peaks

Often a grey chaos erasing the green heights
but now it lies sharp-edged like the great white whale
white as the space between colors
whiter than terror or hope or surrender
beached on the city's breasts
till a lurch of its flukes
sends it down to the sea of the city
which buoys it and leaves us
behind with the Pequod's timbers
from which we shall build a new city
to honor that cloud
one of these days after many of these days

these days of luminous indolence
watchful impotence anxious indifference
(call it gathering strength)
on one side or the other of Meaning—
the cloud the whale is a while's meaning
temptation husk negative image of shadow
and the white whale will churn underneath
soaked in its blood stabbed by absurd sticks
preparing its next wild visibility

while breasts stand green and nippled again
and traffic is bathed in glints from white stucco shells
the light of pines of giant blue eggs of unknown birds

Over the Bay Bridge

Huge the sky and dark as the shadow of a shadow

The bridge: beads shining tightly across the neck of the
 sky
Is there another end beyond the arch the edge?
The bulge in my throat?

Hanging over the hump of the night—

Beyond the arch
The sudden electric city floats
Incontrovertible empty eyes
Shimmering ghost city
Suspended between black and black
Home! home! There is no home like the central glow
In a black pool stretching the skin of eyes

I want to stop and reach across to kiss the city skin
Not much traffic but law is law

So inescapably down to the nearing shore
Down a ramp
Under the skin
No longer a shore, no longer afloat
But a fixed place of steel and glass light
Billboards usurp buildings
Buildings usurp sky

Buzzsaws to the starless night!
Pyramids to the living dead!
Razor blades in the sky's neck!
Fluorescent tombs for the administration of far regions!
Slabs of congealed labor!
Beautiful!
                And the light freezes

Find something to praise if you can
All right

Praise to emptiness in the city skull
Praise to extinguished boardrooms
Praise to lustrous sulphur crystals before they ignite
Praise to memory of hovering light in the middle space
And now all praise to sleep
                            in a small apartment far from
                            light

The Sky Downtown

The sky begins here,
at the rim of my fingers, which rise
of their own accord, which do not cling now.

The sky begins here
and pulses without a sound to a place
we call "there," which is everywhere.

It is not the fault of this sky
that it gets interrupted
by razors of glass and steel

which are wielded not
by the need to pierce the sky
but by what they call "real estate values."

Accidental, then. The accidents
of men, the squandered cities.
If I look away, when I look

beneath my fingers, at times
I can see the sky here, too,
between my hand and the street,

between my hand and that hand of yours.

In Mendocino County

Sweet is the soundless road
as a spider scurries, stops, scurries across

Watchgeese hiss
Puddle of milk in the golden mud

Silent funeral caravan winds through the fog
on its way to a christening

Siberian husky roams
looking for mate

*

Innkeeper feeds the freebooters
who claim they can smell a straight

and talk about buying land and guns
and wander into town for whores

New pioneers
New chewing gum stuck under the counter

*

At the fringe of the beach:
"BOISE CASCADE TREE FARM

"Only God can
    make a tree

"and trees were
    made for use

"protect young trees
    for future use"

*

I am here, she is here
We talk about the ways we didn't talk

Misunderstanding on sand soil
The sun burns through our feet

Giant ego stalks through the pygmy forest
If it falls and nobody hears, it makes a sound

Morning in Santa Barbara

Green, green, wintersoup green,
green as the unripe melon of renaissance hope,
green of the hothouse melting into the sun,
evergreen, cactusleaf green,
undersun green, underwear green,
green splicing the night and the broken celluloid day,
green blur of the ever-returning pages of forbidden books,
green as the shadow of waiting,
melted green in the jello of squandered nights, trying to
    set,
frozen green in the lukewarm muscular wind,
green of revived grapes,
green gone to white around oranges,
green as the sour apple of heart's recollection,
green as the rug on the toilet-bowl cover,
green as the teeth of wretched prophets,
green gone vaguing into shadowy light.

Through Wyoming

flat-bottomed clouds over the sand.
thoughtflakes fall dissolve into the warm sand.
mesas buttes what's the difference?
rock faces of unelected presidents:
red faces, lost and found in the tribe,
creased and refound, haunting the way across.
lush browns under unbounded sky.
the waitress and I equally small.
Equality State.

flagwomen wave us past the progress patch.
smile long and languorously.
a long path.
flagwomen! under the mesas buttes.

love of land!
unpopulated.
not responsible
for property. for seizures.
deserving grapes.
unneeding of them.
sun shines through the rock.
requited love. and I am lost and refound.

why?
              om   ing
why   ommmmm   ing

sweet air. juice of jade across my split lips.
and the land is fenced away—
true enough. and false.
one may love unpopulated land and justice at the same
    time.

land parts for traffic and rejoins:
how to rejoin the land without and within?
rejoin the mindbody's planet, cliffs of the spirit,
sand of the heart, faces carved in our own rock?

all right. I See America Now:
tomorrow may be too late.
but I am warm and transparent:
turbulent chunks flakes of thought dissolve in me,
pass through like warmed light.

and when I stiffen and break the rays and waves
that want to pass lightly through, slightly transformed—
when turbulence turns opaque, as it surely will,
when the glass bowl of sky shatters,

behind the shards is another big blue bowl.

Big Thompson River

Ceaseless. Rushing.
No hurry. Over and over the rock.

My thoughts overlap, of grave mistakes.
Rushing. Hurry. And in me, suddenly,

silence, grave and implacable
as the rock in the center of rapids.

My ears sit by the rock, unhearing
the rubbing away of rock.

*

Too much effusing:
I rise and walk under the grey-bronze cliffs.

Flowers. Scents. Gentler flowing.
I'm separate but not alone.

Seeing! Sharp lines, light within leaves,
color sharp on the tongue.

Revival of sense: precondition
of survival.

*

Where now are the flowing words,
the standing word-rock?

*

Evolution drives the brain, they say,
from simple to complex

but consider entropy:
from noise to silence, stream to rock.

In the beginning was a scream:
more screams; then, at times, silence carved in screams.

*

Slip away, slip half-under,
let the water overrush.

Stand among:
dampened and intact.

Trail Ridge Road, Rocky Mountain National Park

It begins as forced awe:
pines limp across the scorched rock,
the tiny tundra flowers, yellow, blue,

mushroom rocks are shelters for wizened eyes,
wisps of cloud screening the full circle of peaks:
enormity beyond any scale I can grasp,

another kind of space, my eyes slumping down
to the trail, withering with years of matter-of-fact
enormities I've faced without facing,

and I know the terror is in the habit
of living in the chinks between illusions.
And so I force myself to bathe in reverence

despite my blood's fear—
until the clouds break and drift apart,
a blue skylight opens in the roof of the world

and the mountains move like silent thunder.
My doubt thins with the air,
everything looms as shape, sufficiency, pure form,

the mushroom rocks are growing things,
there is no down, only up
and across, only the same direction,

there is *here* in valley, rocks, peaks: one body
on both sides of my porous, revived skin.
Awe sinks into my bones like the mountain mist—

through my bones, draining
into the soil, leaving me dizzy.
—When can I stand more than a little God?

New York on a Mild Day

When I lift my eyes from the traffic,
from the driven crowds of the random ones,
the rush of hours and the hours
of waiting on corners and benches
for a glimpse of a clock without hands,

when I turn my ears from the paper wind,
from the whine of berserk buildings,
the hammer of heels, the roar of wheels,
the talk of chances and the talk of none,
the talk of crime and the crime of talk—

in a thin slice of sky between spiked cliffs
I see dubious angels riding the wind.

Through Nevada

A giant neon cowboy greets us
at the Utah border—bearers of money,
bearers of wilted bodies.

By the light of scrub and papier-mâché sky
there is nothing left but jokes,
awkward exercises of mind

against the odds—
dust full in the face.
There is nothing to do but pass

or be passed, pass through
the land of fast bombs,
and in the casinos

slow bombs endlessly ticking.
If you do not avert your eyes,
just often enough

you see the machines spit nickels:
mainline manna for the next-to-last chance
as if it could finally be the last.

Dredge the eyes up, away, away—
where even the clouds clink
like bored slot-machine eyes.

This state's not big enough
for the AEC and the Mafia
and Howard Hughes and us:

Our bumper sticker reads:
CALIFORNIA AND BUST.
My mind is a daylight fire in the desert.

Outside as Inside

What's the Matter America

What's the matter America my shaving lotion smells limp
What's the matter America it snowed in San Francisco
    today
What's the matter America the starving eyes of children
    have been blacked out all over the country because
    the game's being played in every town
What's the matter America the flagpole's been chopped in
    half so there's nothing higher now than half-mast
What's the matter America the tar and nicotine content
    is shrinking but I'm still dying
I'm going to get Herbal Forest lotion
What's the matter America the toilets are flushing up
    broken bones
What's the matter America the continents are still drifting
    apart
What's the matter America the couples are breaking up
    like ice but it's not spring
What's the matter America the hands were torn off the
    clock but it's still ticking
What's the matter America the national parks are
    closed to bears
What's the matter America money costs more and more,
    too much
What's the matter America it's raining syringes
What's the matter America rats are exported from the
    wharves
What's the matter America smoke is rising to feed the air
    conditioners
I think I'll try lemon-lime
What's the matter America I'm missing myself, I've been
    gone all these years

America are you the face on the other side of the two-way mirror
What's the matter America that shape in the dark with a knife is your fugitive mind
What's the matter America Henry Kissinger is sharing a sofa with Madame Binh but he can't seduce her
What's the matter America everyone's waiting in line and there's no front
I'm sick of menthol

What's the matter America I'm vomiting iron bars
I'm getting crazier if you're outside why are you knocking from inside where do you stop
America I'm wrestling with myself can I win
What's the matter America the alarm has been ringing constantly where is the finger to turn it off my finger doesn't work is it time to wake up yet
America my psychiatrist rejects me my guru got mugged the other day
America get out of my head who invited you
What's the matter America I've heard all the explanations I believe them capitalism male supremacy egotism fear but why

America I came here for the waters I was misinformed
America you're always doing the thinking for both of us
America we all try you succeed
America of all the gin joints in all the world you have to walk into mine
America I'm sick of being the usual suspect

What's the matter America eating has become harder there are parasites in the plates the plates taste like a swollen tongue there's a small corpse in the freezer the bananas taste like yellow skin there's flesh in the toothpaste tube I found a tooth in the hamburger and it wasn't mine the organic honey tastes like last month's milk last month's milk tastes like last month's body count and they're talking about peace the flag out the window is all gristle dissolving in oxides of nitrogen and sulfur what's the matter America I'm eating from an ashtray

What's the matter America I'm lost in a kaleidoscope of
    despair aren't the colors interesting are you bored
America every time I get close you're out of reach you
    rocket away
America you're eating my friends why don't you throw up
    don't we stick in your throat yet
America I've sent in all the coupons entered all the sweep-
    stakes prayed appropriately watched the Super Bowl
    what has it got me
America getting back at you is like punching a lake
I'm not Allen Ginsberg but you're still America
America go down as fast as you want but I'm not going
    with you I don't know where I'm going but I'm not
    going with you

The General's Nightmare

The land is crisp black, and glows like coal
as my helicopter descends through a glittering tunnel.
I am marching under an archway made of antlers.
My saluting hand sprouts a point
and stabs my head. I inspect the troops.
Their socks don't match. "Men!" I say,
"You're under arrest!" They turn into goats
and frisk away. My copter sprouts wings
and takes off, screeching. I pursue the goats
and stub my foot on a diamond. I crush it
to dust. An enlisted man runs up. "Thank God
you're not a goat," I say, and reach
for his hand. He grins and throws his rifle
at my feet: it turns into an Erector set.
"These are your orders." He hands me a sealed envelope
made of dark skin: "Proceed to the valley
immediately." The envelope shrinks
into a packet of sugar. My pistol boils in my hand.
I crawl to the valley. My knees are torn. I drink
my own blood: it tastes like scotch. "Stand up!"
a man says. He reminds me of an old friend
I never wanted to see again. "I'm glad you've come,"
he says. "Come see your home. March!"
I drag my feet through a gantlet of Sioux
women.

Oobie Doobie

> *For Carol Feraci, a member of the chorus line of the Ray Conniff Singers, who, just before a White House performance for Mr. and Mrs. Nixon and the founders of* Readers Digest, *stepped forward and denounced the war to the President's face. To reporters afterward she described herself as an "oobie-doobie-doo girl." (January 28, 1972)*

She used to scissor her legs, present
her skin on a salver, she belonged
in the special places with the special silver,
a dinner decoration, a slice of dessert.

Dispenser of bland pleasure in a mobile
massage parlor for bad faith
holds up a sign: "Stop the Killing."
"Bless the Berrigans and Daniel Ellsberg."

Consternation in the East Room,
Nixon stretching his smile taut
over wire frame, and the singers shout,
"Throw her out." She leaves the room,

the special silver, the bone-white house,
steps off display and out of her costume.
Sing oobie-doobie, oobie-doobie,
oobie-doobie, all a-rooty.

"U.S. Attempted to Ignite Vietnam Forests in '66-67"

"MISSOULA, Montana, July 16—Well-informed civilian and military sources have disclosed that in an effort to clear away enemy-controlled forests, the United States made a number of concerted attempts to set huge fire storms in Vietnam during 1966 and 1967. The project was ultimately abandoned, they said, because the moist tropical rain forest would not burn.

The project was undertaken with the collaboration of fire-prevention experts from the United States Forest Service. . . .

A forestry contingent, working under contract to the [Pentagon's Advanced Research Projects Agency], was believed to include Craig Chandler, now in Washington as director of forest-fire research for the Forest Service. . . ."

The New York Times,
July 21, 1972

Smokey the Bear crouches over an aerial map.
Wearing madras shorts Smokey the Bear studies the map.
There are different colors to enjoy.

Smokey the Bear has been to school.
He has a problem-solving attitude.
He sticks pins in the aerial map.

Smokey the Bear stretches his paws.
He is restless.

There is pounding in the forest.
Smokey the Bear is nailing bamboo to a cross.

It remains bamboo.

Smokey frowns and gathers kindling.
Smokey lights up a Parliament with a recessed tip.
He leans down to the kindling with his Zippo.

Smoke gets in his eyes.

He rubs sticks together.
The bamboo does not burn.

He hires consultants who have been to graduate school.
They are experts on fire.
He gives them a cost-plus contract.
They curse the dampness.

Smokey puffs on his Parliament with its recessed tip.
He studies the situation through Cool-Ray sunglasses.

He sighs.
He shrugs.
He curses the limits of knowledge.
He picks up his shovel and goes back to putting out fires.

Wallace Shot

A fool has dumped another martyr in our groaning ditch.
Sympathy wrestles with horror. . . . Only the guns come
   easy.
Only the guns wait in stores for the instant redemption
of quiet men with nothing else to point
when merely pointing the finger is like staring at yourself,
it changes nothing. The loners, quiet men, lurkers
are making history the only way they know how.
The boy who told me the news, a crossing guard
nonchalant in his uniform, wished it had been Nixon,
but was still excited enough. The woman who gave me a
   ride
was happy, though she granted shooting was not the way.
So much excitement! like the rapt expressions
of bored passers-by taking in the demolition
of old buildings. At least something happens,
but the wrecking-ball swings and pounds in the pit
of our churning sideline stomach. Wait and see:
the martyr will make the silence scream,
while most of the loners learn to huddle in barracks
and a few examine the daily papers page by page
for incomprehensible suitable targets. . . . The news is out:
Wallace will live. Am I still breathing?

Nixon

He pulls his own strings: the mouth opens
revealing the teeth of a tomb.

> In the long summer of Whittier
> a boy delivers papers, not
> knowing why he is sad.

Long life to the work ethic, intones the man
who shuffles lives on paper.

> Along Lake Michigan, boys dream of taking
> potshots at the stinking fish.

Bile is sieved through flannel,
distilled into Civilization.

> Behind the gas station in North Dakota
> the young men pick their teeth, waiting
> for demolition derby.

The stench of confidence rises from the mouth,
and other eyes tear.

> On the other side of the world, peasants
> move like feathers through the paddies.

Gray matter slides into the air,
lime of lies that destroys the evidence.

The McGovern Campaign

After the dry spring,
the shrinking reservoirs and the blighted trees

and the fervent ritual dance
learned from books with half our thirsting hearts

came the sudden bulging clouds,
the summer thunderstorm

and I held my mouth open, my head tilted
back, and my thirst remained.

There on the ground is an old bucket,
rusty and leaking.

They say it is rusty and leaking.
I see it is rusty and leaking

and know that rust is not lethal
and know this is the only bucket in the rain

and will run over.
Drink.

The Defeated

The winners are twirling pinwheels
they call history. In the shock

of the full moon they seem themselves gloriously
blind in the glare of some unknown ocean.

The winners own Picasso's clown. They hire
Quixote as a tourguide, and quote Pascal.

The winners sell a franchise
for despair, and take home the profit

and reinvest. The winners sometimes lose,
and call it winning. Everyone reads

their books, and many believe them. The reviews,
uniformly favorable, are written by winners.

The winners will go to Hell, winning,
drinking the finest vintage from new skulls,

while the defeated ascend on bloody hands and knees,
on stone, standing only long enough to stumble,

to stand, perhaps, one day on another plane
triumphant in oblivion.

Hiatus

This interim, postpartum grace
descends from sudden skies,
and for being doomed is all the more
precious, like flowers awaiting bombs,

like life itself. This space
between the sentences, call it
happiness, evasion, triumph,
simple peace, is here,

not its fault
if peace amounts to hiatus,
the smooth skin between
patches of rash on the earth's flesh.

Was there ever a peace
that didn't prepare war?
that didn't pace in the anteroom
waiting to take its place

with the defense
before a faceless judge?
Well, this silence is a time
for exercises in devotion,

isometric training in the simple
most difficult strengths,
and love of what remains, of what begins,
more difficult than love

of what is lost. And when the time
comes, may the knife fall
in the vast spaces
between electrons.

The Seventies

Everyone wants to escape, or else
escape from escaping. Work to buy escape

from work. Duty to flee flowers
to flee duty. Life and death,

pleasure and pain, each eluding the other.
Or call it survival, or even,

with a flourish, awareness,
or even—this is a big one—

transcendence. Hard to say
where is beyond and where is simply away.

Is it freedom we escape, or is
what we call freedom the escape?

Prisoners who hoard spoons and scrape tunnels,
wardens away on vacation—all, all plotting

and if there are enough of us, the world
will flee from itself at the speed of light

leaving itself to no one. Know what I escape
and you shall know me, this is the motto.

America, among other things,
worn way past the shine,

unraveling in stench, nothing to wear.
Or are there blossoms and giggling skies?

The Chief Samurai

> Kurosawa, *The Seven Samurai*

"I've had plenty of experience in battles.
Losing battles, all of them."
He listens to the farmers
besieged by brigands, pleading for help.
Rubs his hand over his stubble hair
and gets to work.

Four out of the seven dead.
After the battle: "Again we've survived."
The singing farmers who feared their hired samurai
turn back to themselves, glide the rice into the water,
into the soil. "Again we're defeated.
The farmers have won. Not us."
Will the warrior ever farm?

He thinks: "I have fought all my life—for what?
For something called honor. Someone called myself.
And for them, the weak and preoccupied.
Whatever I want is not theirs to give.
I lose the joy of homelessness
when my life is my sword protecting their homes.
They hired me. I need them. My loss is my winning.
May I find endurance and cunning to lose well."

His sword is his glory, his glory his lot.

And the rice will rise.

Two Aging Revolutionaries Meet in a Cafe: Fragment

"It was not for nothing. The wheel turns
a notch, the backs bend an inch, harder,
the harsh rope digs into the shoulders,
the wheel creaks a notch
and the backs hold, hold,
to keep the wheel from slipping back,
and hold, and hold. It was not for nothing."

"No,
not for nothing. But it was to be for everything."

"The illusion of the damned. Your everything
is the underside of nothing. One always starts
somewhere. The journey always continues—"

"Over the rancid corpses lining the road, those who died
for bread, for somewhere to go, for something—"

"Not for everything. There were mistakes. Their blood too
has the dignity of sacrifice, of lingering kisses,
the gift of sighs—"

"Of those who did not live
to see the tyranny of bread. And I, and you,
we lie beneath the wheel, trampled
by the blood-lust of slaves
swinging their manacles, and those who speak
for slaves, on the backs of lullaby-chanting
slaves. And where is the wheel that turns for us?"

"We survive. Our backs give out but we survive."

"Cripples, all, crippled by our passion.
Look: we the doctors spread the disease,
we enshrine the ancient crimes. Bitterness works
for survival as well as hope."

"It's not a question
of hope, it's a matter of facts achieved. The journey
of a thousand miles begins with a single stumble."

"Another, and another. What you call facts
are the bitter grounds of dreams,
the residue of the Absolute. Revolution
is a butterknife made of butter."

"Which cuts
when the butter is soft enough, when the knife is hard."

Break-up

Loneliness

I can tell spring will come late this year.
How do you know whether you're finding yourself
or losing me? The same thing, I suppose,
or don't you know. I said go well,
remembered my endless speech, my amplified
silence hanging metallic over the crowd,
you wandering on the fringe of the crowd
looking to sit beside a fountain,
sitting after the crowd has scattered.
My threat melts, my weight dangles,
the words I would speak are hollowing, hollow,
an empty pillow accuses my life.
The roof is rotting. My steps plop
on the wood floor. Go well.

When we laughed together the snowfall lavished
a faint grace upon us. It wasn't the snow
alone, but a kind of loving within our stuck
couple, something moving beneath the freeze.
Now the sound of your skin against mine
is a fading squeak, a lava of absence
rolls over the house, covers me up to my hips,
my hips burn, and I don't remember
why I let myself laugh. Go well.

Now I spot the old Italian man of the street
who sweeps up a week's debris that the city leaves,
who stares and brushes his moustache. Hello.
My companions, Tchaikovsky, Prokofiev,
and Sibelius also make snow sentimental.
Every decent book I read seems desperate.
I'm all wrong, like an unprinted negative.
How many times will I write this poem?
Go well, go well, go well, come back.

Abortions

Walking with mittens into the bland woods of the blank
    spring
where birds and poets twitter for no apparent reason—
I sit on an everyday shore without a name.
Savage condoms and worn tires slide past
and the rest of the rubber garbage. What else,
I think of you, us, the children walking
on vanished beaches, climbing explored rocks,
and the white picket fence of a future
that for not being chosen still hangs in the air.
The hinge of today with tomorrow
buckles and tears loose. The soft
sharp edges of torn brass.

We stalk the abandoned window deep in the woods,
each of us outside, each of us inside,
touching the same pane, wiping away
our winter breath, seeing our noses flat,
our comical looks: "Who, me, the child? Here?"
On opposite sides of this glass we spun like frozen silk,
in common we have the glass
and blondness, cups of light that pour across.

You gather yourself into your shoulders, into your bones.
You have to go. I have to grieve.
Grief on both sides of the glass,
the pure grief that finally finds a name:
all of that which learns not to be born.

Our unborn babies twist in a liquid sleep.
My fist rattles the hard rice in my heart.

Fault

It's your fault, I said
Not me, he said,
You

It's your fault, she said
Not me, I said,
The society

It's our fault, we said
Not us, we said,
The society

And the society said nothing

Five Days Gone

I painted the bedroom walls with silence.
Jim and Janie invited me to dinner.
I was hypnotized by a lousy
Bogart-Greenstreet flick on the tube.
I told Steve I wonder if I'd feel better
if they ended the war.
I forgot to go to the bank.
I remembered to water the plants
and slept till two this afternoon.
I gave the walls a second coat.
Brussels sprouts are still out of season
and I almost bought a can of Hollandaise sauce
until I read the label. I did buy scallops
to treat myself. The price of milk is up
and I couldn't see across the bay today.
I just scraped the corners of the windows.
There are a thousand poems for missing you
and now there are a thousand and one.

I See Us at a Back Table

I see us at a back table in a nightclub with a tuber-
 cular band
where carousing heroes and failures try to remember
 wartime songs,
their mouths curling around the rind of lemon words.
The only tangerine in the house is between our lips.

I see us hitching across the slight hills on a tractor,
slow enough to get where we want to go,
asking naive questions about alfalfa
and hearing only the driver's pop song and the wind.

I hear us laughing for no apparent reason in the
 wind-blown bleachers,
puffing as we race across the empty amphitheater.
Across the field discarded programs scoot and shudder.
Into a disconnected microphone we kiss.

I hear us rustling under the eucalyptus,
useless except to each other, refusing to ask
of each other what we still demand of the world
in elastic words that stretch with overuse.

I see us addressing picture postcards to Christ, Mozart,
Marx, and Doctor Freud, with carbons to the major papers
and radio stations. We write in yellow and red and blue,
"Having a wonderful time. Wish you were here."

Christ is not real, nor Mozart. Only you and I
and a few billion others are real, and we barely.
Shall we run into the night like a mountain stream?
You write me perfect letters saying: "Not now."

The Abandoned Ones Speak of Their
Distant Lovers

We stir the shaken beaten stuff of love affairs, as if
   the stirring
Would make a golden chain between us, as if the talk
Would drive the jeweled pain deep into a sunken chest,
To be sorted through slowly over tea, over a long
   afternoon,
After the long excavation. A letter from her lover,
Former lover, sometimes always lover:
                                       He loves her
Like the sun, the stars, the Vietnamese, etc.:
   transcontinental love
That meets somewhere in a dry Kansas field
Outside the nervous towns.
                          And because he loves,
Or loved, so purely,
He skipped with practiced nonchalance over a small
   matter,
In other words he lied about the other woman.
The guard directs his life's traffic. An acid silence
Composed of words eats through the tin cans of reliability.
Grand are the lyrics of love inscribed on the tombs of trust!

She and I, the abandoned ones, exchange our small
   misshapen vegetables
Of solace, hard-grown in stony soil—the green wisdoms
   of the weedy gardens
Of what we call the heart. Speak of love that will not quit
Despite all mitigating knowledge of clotted Latin names,
Sharp edges, nettles, thorns. Love despite acts!
Love the faithless faith! Love that forgives even love's
   disguises,
Even the loss of love!
                      And you and I, we also loved and
   somehow love
Each other, forever love like the great meadow light
Of the almost permanent stars, light that dignifies
   darkness,
Light of sun among suns, double stars that go their
   chartless ways—
Light that rarely shines these days on the dust of everyday
   dream-scraps.

What do we imagine about each other now
After such farewells, after such journeys?
The continent buckles between us under the stress
Of mystery no knowledge can dispel.
The fragrance in my nostrils today is scent of my own herbs,
This I know, but I smell you still.

And I know when we love so much, and wrongly, we defy our tiny powers,
Love much more than we are able, until we thrash about
In our own sweat. When we love so much
The great word-statues slip and slide
On the edge, actions fall like sediment to the bottom.
Into the great round wonder of love imagined if not lived,
Simplicity sinks and sticks in a sweet mud—
From which, however, the most brilliant plants push up.

Love lived—everyday love that pursues questions as if they were answers;
Love of soft soiled flesh and love's chores, love between the silences
Of compromised passion; the small carings, enormous mistakes,
The trembling fingers and halting hands—
Love lived is a bargain with the absurd, a tangle of motives and chances,
Profusion of charms, confusion of selves,
A pineapple pizza. The only thing simple, though, is death, if that.

After too much talk of too much love, we shrug:
So what's the point of love?—But that is not the question.
We eat in order to eat.

"We May Not Have Much Time," Said He

"We May Not Have Much Time," Said He

"We may not have much time," said he,
  "Let's gambol while we can."
"I've heard that line before," said she,
  "You're just another man."

"It's not the same this time," said he,
  "You know I love you, dear."
"I must confess you're nice," said she,
  "But why not wait a year?"

"A year would be too long," said he,
  "We dangle on the brink."
"We shouldn't go too far," said she,
  "I must have time to think."

"That time may not be ours," said he,
  "These are abnormal days."
"Perhaps you're right; it's strange," said she,
  "My mind is in a haze."

"That's not hard to believe," said he,
  "These are the times that try. . . ."
"All right! Enough! I know!" said she,
  "If you go on I'll cry."

"The time for words is past," said he,
  "I want a little kiss."
"There's nothing more to say," said she,
  "It's never been like this."

    . . . .

"You know, my dear, I lied," said he,
  "To lend an urgent air."
"To tell the truth, my love," said she,
  "I knew and didn't care."

(with apologies to e.e. cummings)

July Night

Convention bleats into the room
Rhetoric passing through our bodies
Nutriment and waste
Neither without the other

Our conversation in new words
Filed clean of rust
Skins dispel the mist
Of habit grown between the skins

And conversation without words
With natural secretions
Sweat and stuff of love
Of partial antidotes

Skins without sweat
Like words without confusion
Despite frequent baths
And tongues' purifications

Smiles pull like sweaters over our doubt
The screen dissolves into the skin
Skin into entire insurrection
A fan blows us high into July night

The Texture of Kumquats

The poem was to begin, or end, "This life
is a testament to life"—the words were clogged
like shit, and anyway who needs them?
Meanwhile night foreclosed the day
and we stepped out to the store, flushed, for the hell
of it, for something roughly the texture of kumquats
—papaya juice and artichoke hearts,
as it turned out—and happened upon
a guy with a gleaming backpack, who timidly asked:
"Do you know the way to Haight and Ashbury?"
As well as I know the way to Grant's Tomb!
I left my metaphysical discontents tucked in his pack
and tinkled with spare change of fear in my pocket—
after fear comes clarity, and then where will I be?
Home again, lovely dull home, the necessary reek
of domesticity, home that—Look, I'm teetering
on the rock of your brown shoulder!

Afternoon

Afternoon is as good a time as any
for making love. The light of your body
across the room, the light of the street,
the light of my last cigarette,
these lights we give and take, inseparably,
and the light of our clothes carelessly dropped
to the floor, at random and purposeful—

afternoon, a small privilege, while the work of the world
goes on, and on, we roll together, never to know
whether our feelings are separate as our bodies,
as a truck accelerates and washing is hung to dry
across the street, you and I

in contact and separated like double stars
compounding lights and shining
hours later, while the house-plants grow

and skin peels away to layers and layers below,
somewhere the skin melts
into unexplored pools of feeling
where eyes cannot reach, unexplorable,
somewhere on the banks of liquid silence
a touching, an I-am-yours

and the long long canyons of our satisfied bodies

and the casual way we put on our clothes
as if we had known each other longer
than the season of green trees,
suspended like a swaying rope bridge
high over a chasm of rock.

This is a now with windows
from which we may peer a few yards
to the other side of the street,
to another house where living goes on
and plants grow with the quiet whirr of the afternoon,
where typewriters clack like woodpeckers,
where one electric guitar summons a band

down to the street where trucks pass
like reptiles from pit to pit,
and the roofs are full of whirling dancers
distracting the drivers

and the mailman passes bringing the wrong letters,
but never mind, his eyes are bright with solace
like yours, giving the world for what you receive—

It doesn't matter that we have lost
original loves, or it does matter,
the windows are filmed with soot,
there is soot in the room, soot on my crotch,
the day is drowning in sweat—

The windows remain open, a breeze passes
through your hair like the afternoon,
breathes with you into the mouth of the day.

Ten Movements

1

Odd, I remember you in lace,
pale blue lace everywhere but your smile.

2

Your illuminated coffee table
is an unfinished manuscript
of something large and unfinished.

3

Because you love the thirteenth century
I try to imagine who I might have been:
a glum rabbi known for an unpredictable wink.

4

Nostalgia is our substitute for hope.
The problem is to choose the appropriate past.

5

If this were the thirteenth century
I would make for you a tapestry
of unicorns surrounding a man.
And in the sequel, no unicorns,
only a man in the middle of a field, in reverie.

6

About hope: the only thing to hope for
is hope itself.

7

What if the history of the sweated-away lives
could leap from the books and swell
into this interim night and sing to us
of soft cloth and the promise of peace?

8

Play only the bass notes of the organ,
you are yourself the deep treble.

9

When night savored morning on its tongue,
long on its long tongue,
and your watch stopped,
the correct time was not missed, or
rather, it is always the correct time.

10

Now it comes clear, I remember you in white,
stepping out of a dark cloud in long sleeves of white,
the nightgown of a dream.

Autumn

The leaves enrich the soil,
presumably.

An ending is also a start,
so they say.

You begin at my outstretched fingers,
perhaps.

Please take me in your arms
and the leaves shall rise to the branch.

Diving

I have been, because of cramps,
water-shy. Still I perch

at the edge of this pool,
kick pebbles into this pool:
soundings, perhaps.

I look down, afraid of toppling,
a tangle of arms and legs,

into my bottomless pool
which is sometimes drained.

You would not have believed
the bottomless could be drained.
I tell you it happens.

Still I perch, watching the ripples.

And now you come up behind me,
your arms surprising and light around my neck,
reminding me I was born a diver.

"Look at your arms," you say,
"your legs!" I look:
I see yours, and the pool is rising,

and you are the ripples.
My toes are clenched,
expectant. My arms
swing back of their own accord.
Look! I'm diving

into your eyes.

A Poem for You in Black and White

All now together soon my love
here somewhere the twining
vines impossible wandering Jews
growing down and up with dancing roots
the stem another root how soon.

For wildest arms and legs most quiet
even sleep is dance and finding
love as grace not consolation here
where sky is neither old
nor new but food distilled of spice.

See the floor is made of thresholds
one after the other
compassionate wood uncomplaining
lasting underfoot. Step please
skip step across the continental floor unclosing.

Color in your eyes and brightly mind
in joy's tranquility. Read
illuminate this manuscript. I send you
sweet Blake's colors dreams truths
fine boldest lines. Illuminate.

Shadows, Rivers

     I'm stumbling, stalking,
lurching, careening down a long lonely road
    and I know you walk with me.
        You are my shadow
     and I am yours, and neither of us
is shadowy. We know where the road goes
    and don't need to speak of it.
       Not-yet
     always lover giving eternal
arm
    for arm—
      it's happening now, always now—
under a single sky. I'm not alone
ever, it's only the thin shell of feeling that has me
       caged—sometimes it feels like lead—
    but when I burst through
       you're here on the other side being born
and the other side is within me. I'm leaving
     nothing behind but the shell.

                        Way down below
   hulks of what we call the self
     I'm here with you with all the melodies
        ever sung,
       and those not yet invented: the still
        and rippling tones
    funneling into forever now,
still and rippling under and over the crumbling piers,
     the rotted timbers that shore up the past
    and pass for tomorrow.
                    And listen—
You're not alone, watch
     your shadow it's me,
      that dark river converging with yours is mine,
        that river always converging,
    as fast as need be, as slow,
    into silvery green, always converging,
       ever the same and a different river,
flowing like heat from the fireplace, warming your cheek.

Prologue to Living in the Present

On the Edge

Camping out on the edge is not recommended
to those with bad nerves, and is not required
of anyone else. When stones clatter the long stone way
to something that might as well be bottom,
for all I can hear, my heart stops, and starts again.
There might be something soft at the bottom:
a bed of pine needles, perhaps, lost in mist and distance.

But if there were nothing but rock spikes,
I would hear no different. It's too far down.
Night tilts like gravel over the edge
but night is night and remains the night.
The sky straddles my chest. Who would have dreamed
there could be so many shades of grey? A matter of guts:
waiting with grace among shades of grey.

Why are volcanoes extinct? Where is the absolute lava
to boil and fill the canyon? Glacier, scrape,
scrape the granite, break rock from rock,
hollow the boring landscape! As it is,
the shelf's slide over the edge in a heavy rain
is a regular thing. I back away barely in time.
Always in time.

Rock stands, only my eyes move
to study rock and sky, gradations of grey.
When I tire of wrestling expressionless angels
I fiddle with Coleman stove and metal cups,
stir the worn stew and study the sun through paper
   windows.
The wall is lined with labelless cans. With modern goods
almost any shelf is wide enough for a way of existing.

Guts is the art of waiting with grace
until the crickets make a soundlessness,

I only hear my ordinary heart, and the moment comes
to back down the cliff on loose stones.
Meanwhile I commune with crickets and,
as the sun stupidly rises, I pipe my song.
I pipe my ludicrous song!

In the Desert, Almost Doomed

In the desert, almost doomed,
Where I wandered in my grieving,
The bush burned and was consumed.
I clutched my hand and tried believing.

I sweated half the night, all ripe
For Moses, Mary, or the living.
Finally I fell asleep
And dreamed of hanging men believing.

I gathered my unwieldly pack
And boots and set about achieving
Distance. When I sprained my back
I contemplated disbelieving.

A dune-buggy ambulance
After days and nights of driving
Flew off a cliff. Such events
Are exercises for believing.

It's not the sun that melts my claw
Or moon that tempts me with deceiving,
Only a logic and a flaw:
I disbelieve in disbelieving.

Poem Beginning with "But"

But despite the sun and the moon and the last demonstration
I want to weep.

I doubt my tears would rust the wheels,
derail the careening freight of the National Purpose—

enough if only my tiny frozen eyes could melt
and form again on another shore

but actually I would rather sit on the front porch
dry-eyed in the summer rain,

comment dispassionately on current affairs—
afterward.

A good American boy
of snips and snails and rattlesnake tails

would get used to swallowing hard each stringy bean
like a flagpole.

Neither Steve McQueen nor Kosygin would cry
but stand straight, like a man.

In Muir Woods, under the redwood pillars
I heard a delighted child ask her mother:

"Do they allow crying here?"
—How early they learn to assume nothing in public!

The Old Stadium

So many seats are broken! splinters stabbing splinters,
slats engraving my eyes,
green paint curlicues tickling my eyes—
down here, when green was green and had not gone
    to brown,
the patron gods sent messengers to run in circles
for our delight, and messages were often received.
I haven't heard a message in years, have you?

My eyes swayed up following the white blur of Alvin
    Dark's last fly ball, going, going, even after it went
    foul, like stitched manna into the other kid's eager
    terrified hand;
And the third baseman, what was his name, snatched the
    grounder short and clean and skipped once, twice
    toward first, saucily waiting as Duke Snider hustled
    toward first oblivious, and then the arm cocked and
    the ball cracked like a shot into the big mitt, and the
    ump's thumb stuck up like a dog's ear, and I was
    content;
And when big Ralph Kiner waited at three-and-two and
    Willie stood 420 feet out, at least, in center, and Kiner
    blooped the ball over second, and Willie came soaring
    like an angel, glove outstretched, and dove, and lost
    his cap, of course, and came up with the white prize,
    and I was content.
You don't remember. I can hardly remember.

All the empty roofs!
the neighbors walled off, tier below tier,
raging discreetly against the windows.
The infield is littered with faded programs, hot dog
    wrappers,
Captain Marvel comics, Mr. Potato Heads,
the dugout stuffed with rusty erector sets.
I stand on the pitcher's mound
and throw a dirt strike into the wind,
the wind blows it back in my face.

If the past didn't exist we would have to invent it.
The past doesn't exist. Only monuments
and ancient traps and capsules
and the roar of a crowd that seems to be past
as if the ocean were in the shell. But what the hell,
let's see if something's buried where home plate used to be,
where thousands of times those feet touched something
    hard
at the end of victorious rounds before the next at-bat.

How Long

How long does it take to go crazy.
My mind is a wild predictable
snail. The pain. The pain.
                         How long.
Soon, or must I wait
till I die. Foaming out of the grave.
Babbling to a stoned medium.
Isn't there death after life.
                         O rare disease!
It's always rare inside the skull,
squeezing here, but when to burst.
Tunnel under the steady waters,
crack in the walls. Depths: no rapture.
                              The weight.
The weight.
          When, where, how to let go
of the outside inside, every calamity creates
an equal and opposite . . . when

too far to come back, and why come back
to weight clenched in the brain, and why
go there, the unforgivable—no, unattainable—
length away, or is outward the way in,

or why not stay right here, clutched in the handicap
like a man in a wheelchair playing ping-pong,
taking, returning whatever comes. . . .
                                    O rare disease!
You too?

Praying in the Bathroom

The sheets were yellow as goldenrod,
my sheets for now, the sheets of an inn,
and I could imagine another head on this pillow
bright as the sun stored in these sheets

and the town was as sweet and rotten as other towns
and the trees flared nearby like vegetable flutes
and the music was raw and too purple
but my ears funneled into my mind and I was revived

until I got up to brush my teeth
and blood poured from the faucet,
somebody's blood, one of those inconvenient
mementoes washing ashore, or the marrow

of small bones, or the ecstatic walking wound,
the gourmet of ground glass, or the overdosed
slaves of the furnace, the darkened diggers
of dead ferns, or the fiery deer

escaping too late, or a lost rat.
Come see the blood in the sink!
the everyday blood soon to be bottled,
transfused for our own wounds

that they shall not have died in vain;
or perhaps it is really rust, it is only *this* old house
that is rusting, and the breeze still blows
the flag of red meat, and the lovers are still

entwined on a bench by the river, and a late-night coffee
enriches the blood of a hopeful monk,
and the poor may awaken to clear water—
maybe it's only me praying in the bathroom,

only my strained porcelain eyes
staring after another dismembered self
who once wandered the greener streets in search of plums
until he sacrificed himself to feed the rat.

Traffic Lights

Red freezes my foot
Green excites joy turning to haste and fear
I speed through yellow

In Massachusetts
Green lights flash on and off, an odd message
For people like me

Foundation

1

One after one the homes come down,
clattering, brick on brick, or
soft like a shirt collapsing onto a chair
after the body is gone.

House goes down: try tent:
tent goes down, dome goes down,
brick, glass, wood go down—

Still the foundation, slab
of plain concrete, flat bottom
under the rubble, lasts.

Again I sit in the middle of a council of pieces,
consult shards, assemble
broken bricks for a new home.

After the scrap is cleared away
concrete is cooling—rough-surfaced, solid,
revealed only after the house is gone.

2

What is longing but a great tree
with many roots thrusting
in and down, up and through

the flat foundation?
Roots of the one world-tree
breaking through

splitting the permanence—
and yet the roots may rise
to become the trees of a newer house,

the shank and shade of an improvised room.

Functions of Imagination

1

When the brick building shakes, when the great storm
rages out of the furnace and sucks oxygen
a tiptoe height out of breathing range, and when smoke

fills the vacated space in a dawn of choking,
when transparency is seared into transparency
and the green sticks to the blue becoming black,

when the floor trembles and flame rumbles
and I swallow the stench and my lungs are scorched
and I fear collapse and, even more, ennui,

I would lie in my mind's idea of a green field.

2

When I lie in a green field,
when the curve of hill swells in my low absorbent eye,
when a tree steals into my mind

and its leaves sway in my seeing-without-having-to-look
   mind—

and when the carpet dissolves and singular blades of grass
fight back and prickle my neck,

and when mosquitoes gather near still water
in the early dusk and I am tired
of grinding them bloody between my palms,

I would lie in my mind's idea of a green field.
In my mind's eye
I lie in my mind's idea

of a green field.

After Newton: Ideological Fruit

I sit under the tree watching apples
turn to lemons, then to pomegranates

bursting. Before I get the seeds to my mouth
they have rotted.

My why slips under the skin of a rounded truth.
Apple = lemon = pomegranate after a while.

My why leaves a hole in each
and each tastes like a bruise.

I wonder where the single rounded truth has gone
since once it seemed to hang directly overhead,

ready to fall. In that illusion coiled my why
which crawls, hungry and indiscriminate.

A pillow falls from the tree,
I rest my head.

Trembling

This trembling is the trembling of a tree. Now one, now another branch of leaves sways in its own time.

But I am also the wind.

Now

I want Now. I type
Not.
    Here it is. No,
it's gone.

Now is slipping away
into
    Now. And what I want
is then, or later, not
here.
    What time is it? Now?
Already? I didn't know it was that
Now.
    I want
Now. I type Not.

The Cave

After all is said—not done—here we are in a cave.
The emissary we sent has not returned,

he is probably stumbling around up there,
or maybe he never left. Do you remember?

This ice water that soaks our bones is probably
not his message, it is simply the water of ice.

This business of carrying on, this tedium,
why is it so cold?

Last night I dreamed I loved someone up there,
    and brought her
here. Now her bones are frozen too.

There are many tunnels. You must crawl a long way
to learn if they lead up, or down, or sideways.

Most lead sideways, so it seems.
After all is said—and done—here we are in a cave.

Water

Enclosure. Hard surfaces
moving together. Me in the
middle. Trapped.

Hard surfaces. Through them
some light. If it is possible
to believe in beyond.

And if not light, what is it?
Think above it. Imagine beyond.
Imagine as hard surfaces come, they're coming—

Learn to spread out. Fill
available space. Water
between two panes of glass.

Many patterns to make
and still be water. Preserved
for another day.

Anatomy of Quiet

Quiet! The books I read
disturb my peace.

Each page
is a paper plane waiting to be folded:

a paper bomber
over the huts of my mind's village.

The hell with books!
Quiet! No-reading room.

Listen to the quiet, dissolving
into the sound of which it is made:

there is an engine always running,
idling most of the time.

Dry feet rustle on the sidewalk.
A car strips the asphalt skin.

Now someone is whistling over the street
as if it were a Coke bottle.

A car starts up. The street
is clearing its throat.

Lover

We think something is lost: it *is* lost: it can be found.
Today I gather myself in my arms and greet my long-lost
    lover: myself.
And loving myself I love, for once, neither for how big
    nor how little I am, neither in pity, solace, nor pride.
And loving myself I gather into my arms all who would
    be held, and all who would not be held.
I love in tears not of loss, for once, but of finding:
Tears of the river endlessly filling the sea, mixing with
    all your tears and all the still and bitter tears of the
    world.
Tears of the universe streaming. Tears of the torn
    reuniting.
Tears in which the single song of the world assembles
    itself from broken measures and broken notes.

My skin is that river moving through the streets, moving
    the streets, my feet are tender on the pavement,
    whether the streets know it
Or not. And if you and the streets like plastic coats repel
    my love, now in the last blue of the day
Stars are raining softly over the hills, my tears are singing
    the sweet song that everyone knows—everyone who
    can learn to remember—
Let's say that everyone knows.

Caterpillar and Butterfly

Ambition

Ambition storms the beach
And measures it.

Ambition struts away from the water's edge
To preserve footprints.

After the water washes away the castle
Ambition builds a bigger castle.

Ambition spits in the ocean
And watches the spot.

Ambition gathers the golden sand
In a sieve.

The Ambassador from Misery Shuffles His Feet under the Bargaining Table

I slap my cards on the table. You claim you have what you want. Consider that bliss is ignorance, you are incomplete. Don't you know about—but your eyes gleam in anticipation, you've heard it all, I needn't itemize. The usual horrors, give or take, I enter my list in the record. No doubt you have your own. I only point out my position has the grace and point of realism. Mortality is grim, not this my soul, I only play out my mission with a suitable passion. What you call happiness lacks passion, sir, the final warmth of a skin that must be worn. You escape from the world, you escape from yourself, you escape from the demons, and, my friend, it does not matter whether they are bred in the brain or in the world as it is, the effect at the moment is identical. You are prone to shock when you hear the bad news, whereas I have already heard it, shake my head and take another step in the same swamp. My unshakable knowledge allows me God's gift of doggedness. Suffering is natural as trees, and is, in its heart, after the evanescent causes are stripped away, significant—not more than happiness, it's true, but not a whit less. But lest you think I offer only a choice of meaninglessness, I remind you that without my darkness you would never know light for what it is. If I didn't exist you would have to invent me. One moment, sir. Before your smile betrays your condescension, I remind you that my government like yours has the power of destruction. We coexist, my friend, in a balance of terrified need. I haunt your days. Knowing I exist refutes your happiness as it makes it possible. And yes, I admit, you haunt me too. That is why we may bargain together. You ask what we want. Good, perhaps we can come to terms. My government has instructed me—Listen: I beg asylum.

The Animal Reunion

for John Fahey, guitarist

Night is reprieved. Flies circle around mosquitoes,
mosquitoes around the fallen pillars. In the dusty
    amphitheater
baboons toss their asses at frightened crows.

The antlers leap from the wall, the head
rejoins the neck. Snakes giggle
and crawl back inside their skins.

Corpses of soldiers whistle across the wind.
It is high time for the gay dismay of animal ghosts
under the glass eye of the moon.

Guitar and organ have opened the animal night.
The rhythm quickens and fingers
pluck animals out of silence

and into their dance, one by two by more,
gravely stomping the ground. . . . The rhythm slows,
stately packs and flocks are forming to stalk the dust—

geese promenade with alligators,
wolves with elephants, and the trout are wearing cowbells:
reprieve without a price is the common animality.

Later, when the fingers rest,
as thousands of tigers pace in thousands of cages,
the hamster spins its luminous wheel.

Sisyphus' Dream

"If You're so great," the Devil said,
"let's see You make a rock so big
You can't move it."
                      "Not that old one
again," growled God. "I dream of it
so hard I sweat. The embarrassment
it's caused Me!"
                "Come on, what kind of a God
are You, giving up so fast? Haven't tried
in centuries, I'll bet."
                      "I'm a wise
old God Who knows the score. Some things
you can do and some you can't. Let Me
alone and let Me watch the humans
make fools of themselves. It's an old God's
only joy."
           "You dream of it, You say?
Strange thing to see a God so weak
and dreamy, out of sorts and sweating—"

"Get out of here! You make Me mad!"

"—irascible too. You know, God, could
be time for a new boss running things,
someone—You know—more stable. . . ."
                                      God
got up. "I swore I'd never try
again, but just to show you why Gods
are wise I'll waste my time. Get out
of the way."
                  And God stretched out His arms
and clenched His fists, strained His aging
frame, muttered and groaned, and squeezed
His wrinkled eyelids shut. And then
the rock was there.
                    "It's big, all right,"
the Devil said. "Let's see You move it
now. Don't say You can't."

"It *is*
quite a rock, very impressive. Observe
the texture, the interplay of grey
and white, the curious veins—No need
to be compulsive, Devil. Forget
this crap, stand back and admire the thing."

"You're bound to try to move it, God,
aesthetics are something else. Where's
Your famous will?"
"Do you have to see
it move, don't you know when to stop? I'm God,
and Gods move rocks. That's the way things are."

"Prove it."
"Very well, make fun
of an old God." God leaned on the rock
and pushed. His muscles swelled. The rock
stood fast. He thought the rock was lovely.
He tried again. No change. God pushed
for hours and nothing happened. He thought
perhaps He was not God.
"You're faking,
God. Malingering's as bad
as logical failure, You know."
"Idiot!
Can't you see Me sweat? Just give Me
a little time."
The Devil went out
for a Coke. When he came back, God
was panting. The Devil leaned against
the air, taking a long swallow,
grinning. After eternity
the rock, with a sound of thunder, began
to roll. God shook his head and sighed.
"I've failed," He said. "I cannot make
a rock so big I cannot move it."

"You almost broke my back with Your fucking
rock!" the Devil screamed, sprawled
in the dust where the rock had laid him.

The Hitchhiker Revolts

The day snails across the sky
with him, the shell on its back.

Once, home was the end of the road,
the road was the price of home.

Down the road was an unknown city,
another coast becoming horizon,

his vision shining over the tide,
almost a home under a fixed sky.

Now the side of the road is a hard curb.
Exhaust marks the route on his overused map

torn at the creases.
The sky mocks the road, and also his map.

Brusque farewells stay with him
longer than kisses,

and he envies the owners of fading tailpipes,
the hands relaxed on the steering wheel,

the casual arm over the seat,
the radios oozing loss and wanderlust—

but the last ride, in a remodeled hearse,
left him waiting for a ride.

On the ride before, he was offered a sweet smoke
and was dropped off missing his wallet.

His hand dangles in his lap,
his lap dawdles.

Perhaps he will get used to roadside trees
and undergrowth and occasional meadows.

Days, years: a blur.
He remains unconvinced by trees.

He remains. Under a static sky
he points his cramped thumb,

his dazed V, his fist, and feels
the speedwind of those who leave him behind

and he rests his thumb,
slumped alone by the side of the open road

without a backpack, with only desire
to break the world into brilliant colors.

Ohio . . . the Badlands . . . Yellowstone steam . . .
he squints into the salt flats of imagination

and, shrugging at assembly lines,
thrusts a middle finger at the drivers-by

sealed into their sleek destinations.
He dreams of a backyard furnace

to forge an ugly and useful steel
which may carry him—home?

and gathers himself at last into his legs,
ready to walk the back roads

scouting for wooden inns
and a homesite which is all backyard.

The Day the Clouds Fell

The day the clouds fell
Thunder was a muffled shriek across the sky

The sun pulsed enormous and disappeared
Locusts buzzed the trees' alarm

Rabbits stuffed themselves into their hutches
Chipmunks burrowed barely in time

Whiteness spilled over the violets:
Over the wells, the lakes,

Over the caves in the underbrush:
White-like bleached mud

Light dripped down the gutter
Into a rusty bucket

The clouds fell more softly than expected
According to those who weren't underneath

The Men

As I was saying, says A.,
the thing of it is, I don't
know what I was saying.

Not at all, says B.,
it's exactly like this. What
I was saying, says A.,

is this, or that, it
depends on exactly what
you mean. Which reminds

me, says C., of the time
me and the old lady. Did I
ever tell you, says B.,

about. If you'd let
me get a word in
edgewise, says A.

I surely do, it's a matter,
says B., of. I don't think,
says A., you know what

you're talking. Says C.,
about that time me
and my old. Reminds me,

says A., of what I was
saying. Well, says C.,
sure is good to relax

away from the women.

Seeking

Under every stone
an indentation to be seen as soil.

Behind every curtain
emptiness to be felt as breeze.

With every song
silence to be heard as accompaniment.

After every conversation
a pause to be known as a kiss.

The seeker is not disappointed
in the spaces between the seconds.

The Return of the Repressed

1

Not the upended iceberg, spun
passively by the heavy workings of ocean.

2

The monster of Loch Ness
thrashes out of the water, looks around,
decides to be named a common mammal
or an hallucination, and
sinks, laughing, back in the warm darkness.

3

The dolphin takes leave of its herd,
arcs into the shining air,
a moment of beak and whistle bright
between its herd and its herd
beneath the sea—that moment
its life within its life.

4

The dolphin flashes up, forever
a silver knife sunk deep into the sun.

Caterpillar and Butterfly

"What do I want with wings?
It's dizzy up there, and too easy
Flitting from flower to flower
As if the world were nectar! For others, wings.
For me my tiny legs, but long enough,
Inching over stony ground
Because I belong to this ground,
Because I shall always belong to this ground
And ask no favors. To live is to crawl
Around and over a stone, a twig, a stump;
To keep no records; expect nothing."

"Once I too crawled over the clumped soil
And preferred a twig to destiny. Stone,
Twig, stump, stone, stone: artifacts of plain
Existence: if this and that are not enough,
I reasoned, then enough is never enough,
And there remains the crawl, and only the crawl.
And when—I admit, I admit—I prayed for wings
I also nibbled solace from a few fragrant leaves.
But there are only illusions of choice, concealed in waiting
And prayer, and when the waiting is fat and heavy
There is only the instant at the flower's edge,
The instant between clumps of earth.

                          And then to fly!
I cannot speak of it.
                Do I miss crawling?
Does the day miss the night, or the night the day?
And still, now, there is only the instant in the flower's cave
And the instant before and the instant after."

"There is no instant, only the crawl,
Or the instant is a dot smudged into the long line of
    crawling.
Instants are the luxury of those with wings
To rise above the clumps. When I am here, the spot where
    I am,
I will tighten and learn to get there,
There, there, with the worms, and breathe along the way."

"Crawl, and crawl, and crawl well
And leave the instants sprawling in the dust, and still
You cannot imagine chrysalis,
The long instant that feels like dissolution."

"I await nothing I cannot imagine.
I have heard myths, I have seen wings, and I know myself.
You have forgotten the distances,
The slow crawl measured by body time,
The long day and the long night of time."

"I have forgotten nothing.
We are thinking the same thoughts."

Turning Thirty

After the sleepless journey I made the mistake
of looking back.

I thought I stood at a summit, where breathing was
    strange,
and a summit it was: on the ocean floor.

I made the mistake of looking up.
Between this peak and the next peak is the vast pain.

Start again: I prefer the long and narrow valleys,
where water rests.

Between this valley and the next valley is the vast pain.
Water never rests. Water falls into drops.

I have lived many lives and truths, callings,
throwing off what-they-call careers like outgrown clothes,

dreaming, discarding, moving past
and sometimes through.

People and places last, though changed, and I last too,
driving past myself, a vague shape, a mountain sensed
    in the night.

The sun is an emptiness in the density of form.
Precise ghosts are roasting me on tonight's bonfire.

Unlivable love is locked in a strongbox in my heart.
—If I could dance I'd wheel around myself

and show you unfulfilled faces. Start again:
the huge eyes in the small face are lost, kin are dispersed,

the village exploded. —When I stop to think about it,
you exist, and probably I too. If the losses

scrape down to the lower layers of flesh there are lower
    layers intact,
though it isn't time to speak of healing.

Who writes these lines, after all? Well. . . .
They are written.

My years will detonate the sun. I no longer swim to the raft
to nuzzle my skin against the sun. (Was it ever that way?

Ever a time when things jumped a little with joy
and gold was silent and dreams sifted sweetly through
    my fingers

piling into the delta of all dreams? And light
knew it was light and didn't have to scream?)

Faith is drained, leaving the dregs of dumb hope.
Start again: hope isn't dumb

any more than clothes are dumb in the cold.
—I don't believe it. What I know

is that I count my years like a dog's, seven for one,
which gives me the vantage of centuries

over my buried cities and artifact dreams
and as archaeologist of my past I never strike bottom;

the layers are jumbled together;
the ruins are lovely, as ruins are.

The years have used me as I've used them:
crudely and casually, like a once-favorite toy—

And yet they roll in on me now, warm and constant,
    my years.
I could hug them now, like children lost for a while in a
    carnival crowd.

They come back in the summer nights, and then, sooner
    or later,
go out on their own and grow into strange shapes.

Maybe nothing is lost but the useless memories,
the dead weight of the wrong lessons, as if

experience happened in order to be remembered;
maybe something is lost in order to be found when you
    need it,

like finding a penny on the street
that's fallen out of your own pocket.

I can be washed and soothed in the slow waves of my
    past. It is time
to speak of healing. What's thirty, after all, but another
    number?

—What's 1984? I have scooped myself out and the rest
    is rind.
—No, I shall use my years as tissues for my eyes.

—It isn't time to sum up,
and anyway the adding machines are wrecked. Start again.

Designed by Jon Goodchild.
Straight Arrow Books: Dian-Aziza Ooka, Dennis Kiernan,
Linda Gunnarson, Victoria Jackson, Carol Raṣkin-Ward,
Wendy Werris, Bill Cruz, Rosemary Nightingale and
Alan Rinzler